A Gardener's Guide to Parenting

By Kalo Heldt

WestBow Press books may be ordered through booksellers or by contacting:

WestBow Press
A Division of Thomas Nelson & Zondervan
1663 Liberty Drive
Bloomington, IN 47403
www.westbowpress.com
1 (866) 928-1240

Because of the dynamic nature of the Internet, any web addresses or links contained in this book may have changed since publication and may no longer be valid. The views expressed in this work are solely those of the author and do not necessarily reflect the views of the publisher, and the publisher hereby disclaims any responsibility for them.

Any people depicted in stock imagery provided by Thinkstock are models, and such images are being used for illustrative purposes only.
Certain stock imagery © Thinkstock.

ISBN: 978-1-5127-8390-2 (sc)
ISBN: 978-1-5127-8391-9 (e)

Library of Congress Control Number: 2017905842

Print information available on the last page.

WestBow Press rev. date: 4/17/2017

WESTBOW
PRESS®
A DIVISION OF THOMAS NELSON
& ZONDERVAN

To my wonderful daughters, Trina and Mandy,
without whom I never would have imagined these thoughts.

And to Moms and Dads everywhere who are
facing the challenges of parenting.

Plant flowers where they belong – don't expect marigolds to thrive in the shade or impatiens in the sun.

Allow your child to develop his or her natural talents – an athlete most likely won't become a musician.

Unwanted weeds near a plant will rob it
of nutrients and stunt its growth.

The "wrong" friends will rob a child of opportunities to
practice good behavior and rob him or her of maturity.

When a plant becomes "root bound" it will
stop growing, and will sometimes die.

Children can outgrow rules, so guidelines should be
evaluated and changed or modified when appropriate.

Your greatest time and effort is required
when plants are young - as they become
"established" they will require less work.

Your child requires a lot of time in infancy
and early Childhood - as he or she matures
you will be needed less and less

If you wear thick gloves while working in the garden you will protect your hands, but you will work more effectively with thinner gloves.

If you allow walls to build up between you and your child you will protect yourself from some pain, but it takes intimacy and transparency to parent well.

Companion gardening is a widely accepted practice among gardeners. In the same way that weeds can hinder growth, certain plants grown side-by-side can promote growth and prevent disease.

It is not only important to discourage the "wrong" friends, it is equally important to encourage a good peer group.

*Some of the insects that look the scariest are
the most beneficial to your garden*

*Don't judge your child's friends by their outward
appearance but rather by their character*

Over-pruning can distort a plant, and
in some cases stunt its growth.

Discipline should be appropriate – if you
discipline your child too harshly and too often
you may inhibit or damage his or her spirit.

The birds and the wind may help "volunteers" spring up in the garden, oftentimes enhancing its beauty.

Other adults (relatives, coaches, teachers) will volunteer to influence your child, often adding a new dimension to his or her development.

Proper soil is critical to long-lasting plant growth –
be sure to amend the soil when necessary

Don't select poor soil (school, daycare, activities)
that will keep your child from thriving. If
you are unable to change the situation, be
sure to give extra personal attention.

Relish surprises – when something new springs up in your garden, don't be too quick to yank it out.

Enjoy the spontaneous moments – the conversations and shared experiences that weren't planned are often the best.

Over-fertilization causes burn-out.

Over-scheduling your child will cause burn-out.

If you "dead-head", or pluck off old blossoms, the plant will put more energy into new blooms.

Bury old problems and arguments, thereby providing strength for new growth (and new problems!).

Don't take on a big gardening project when you're already tired – too often that's when accidents occur.

Big parenting decisions shouldn't be made when you're tired – it's OK to tell your child you will make a decision or discuss a situation later.

Thinning is important in fruit production –
otherwise the tree will produce an inferior crop

Encourage your child to do a few things well, rather
than doing a lot of things in an inferior way.

The more time a gardener spends working in the garden, the more beautiful it becomes, and the more pleasure it gives all who see it.

The more time you spend parenting, the greater joy your child will give you and all who come in contact with him or her.

Careful pruning makes a plant healthier and stimulates growth. It should be done on a routine basis.

Caring discipline will enhance your child's development. It must be consistent.

*Fertilize regularly for maximum
growth and production.*

*Expose your child to the "extras" in life on a
regular basis, but not too many at one time.*

Knowledge and hard work can create a
beautiful garden, but nothing can grow without
the sun and water created by God.

A parent's love and hard work can produce a
successful young adult, but to truly flourish
both need a strong faith in God.